T0063911

Talking to
Spirits

Talking to
Spirits

Matthew Oreilly

authorHOUSE®

AuthorHouse™ UK Ltd.
1663 Liberty Drive
Bloomington, IN 47403   USA
www.authorhouse.co.uk
Phone: 0800.197.4150

Published by AuthorHouse   10/13/2014

ISBN: 978-1-4969-8232-2 (sc)
ISBN: 978-1-4969-8233-9 (e)

Mat.   Dear people, please allow me to express myself. I want to write and publish a book. Is a man able to have such privileges in this day and age?

Edna.   You carry on, Matthew. I think you'll do a brilliant job.

Mat.   Brilliant. How do you know that?

Edna.   It's perfect, Matthew. All we have to do is converse.

Mat.   Yeah, but you're just a voice in my head. You're not alive.

Edna.   I was alive once, Matthew.

Mike.   You too make a great duo, but remember, we are a threesome.

Mat [*apprehensively*].   Yeah. Go on then.

Edna.   [*in a strong, distinctive London accent*]. Thanks.

Mat.   No offence, Mike. Mike, shall I leave wastepaper pages for Scott next door? After all, his flat was a temporary booth for letter dropping over the Christmas period.

Mike. Scott did try and claim he was the letter writer.

Edna. What about Katy? She lives there too.

Mike. Katy was in London with her parents.

Mat. Yeah that's right. I remember. [*Pauses.*] Day one trying to give up cigarettes, Edna.

Edna. Yes, Matthew. I wish you all the best

Mike. Yeah, good luck, Mat.

Edna. I reckon, fill a pad and you've got a book. They may try and edit, but it won't have the same flow.

Mat. What if I get writer's block?

Edna. Don't be silly, Matthew. There's endless chatter, hundreds of different avenues to enter. That's for sure

Mat. Sometimes you may be inspired by reading this; other times, who knows?

Edna. That's right. Every line fits in; that's my belief. I have every confidence.

Mike. You want to listen to Edna.

Mat. Nice bit of morale boosting there. Thanks.

Edna. You'll feel so much better once you're past smoking cravings.

Mat. That's what I like about you guys. You always come back with something positive.

Mike. Also, you have to keep this addictive and funny.

Mat. Am I going to Alcatraz today? Or are the police going to leave me alone this time?

Edna. Oh, Matthew, the police are only doing their job. They're not trying to restrict you in any way.

Mat. When I say prison, I mean Priority House Mental Health Hospital.

Mike. They don't believe you're psychic.

Edna. It's only rough at the moment. We can always tweak it here and there, not much though.

Mat. Hopefully those vampire doctors won't contaminate my blood later. Looks like I'm going in. Hospital just called. Call ignored.

Mike. I don't blame you, mate.

Mat. Yeah, you're not wrong, Mike.

Mike. Why not have a pint down at the Toad Rock Retreat tonight. Nice setting.

Mat. Yeah, I'll have some of that.

Edna. I guess the consultant thought better of bringing you in, Mat.

Mat. Maybe my heart will stop beating so fast for now.

Edna. Please don't talk about women being pieces of furniture to manoeuvre. It's disrespectful, Matthew darling.

Mat. Nice coat your dog's got on there, mate.

Edna. Matthew, don't take the coat. It's keeping the dog warm.

Mike. I wouldn't fancy wearing a pink coat if I was that dog. It doesn't go with its fur colour.

Edna. Don't take any notice of that last comment.

Mat. People need to know that, when I said, 'Nice coat,' it was a quiet conversation with myself.

Edna. Matthew, you do come out with the funniest insecurities.

Mike. He's just giving his own character reference.

Mat. We all know there are lines you don't cross.

Mike. Handbags at twelve paces more like, with that shade of pink. Adult? Male? Both of them with a question mark.

Mat. I want people to laugh and enjoy reading as well.

Mike. I think we have the right mixture.

Mat. You are funny, you two. Is that worth putting down on paper?

Edna. No, Matthew. Some chatter has to stay top secret.

Mike. They're going to be wondering what we were talking about now.

Edna. We have to pick and choose the right ones.

Mat. If that's right for you, I'm not arguing. [*Pauses.*] Nice roast dinner up at my mum's today.

Edna. Yes, good nourishment; it'll fuel you for the day.

Mat. This weightlifting is making me sweat. Edna, I've nearly lost a stone.

Edna. Yes, I'll always support healthy living, Matthew.

Mat. I'll tell you, when I talk with you guys, if it don't half make the days fly by.

Edna. Yes, we're top-quality company, Matthew.

Mike. Top. No pun intended by Edna, Mat.

Mat. *Talking with Ghosts*. I think that's what I'm going to call the book. What do you reckon, Mike?

Mike. Definitely worth jotting down.

Edna. Yes, it's one to remember, Matthew.

Mat. If this book does as well as I'm crossing my fingers it does, life really does begin at forty.

Edna. Yes, in your case, it's absolutely true.

Mat. No counting chickens before they hatch.

Mike. No, that's right, mate. Keep a level head.

Mat. No popping champagne bottles yet.

Edna. Now come, Matthew, exposure can take years in the writing field.

Mike. That meat in your fridge – eat it off the bone, please. There's still plenty on it.

Mat. But I feel like a caveman consuming it like that. [*Changing the subject.*] Kelly said that psychic writing is spooky to Chris.

Mike. You're an original twenty-first century man.

Mat.   Those police officers turning up last night was a bit close.

Edna. They were only showing that they care.

Mat.   Nice bag of dog's mess in the pathway; charming.

Edna. Going over to your sister's for a barbecue?

Mike. Perfect day for it.

Mat.   Yep. Time to fill my boots with free food. [*Looking out the window.*] There goes Sue on her mobility scooter.

Edna. Matthew, I hope you're not trying to get a cheap laugh out of Sue's disability.

Mat.   No, of course not.

Mike. Even Manchester United fans think Steve was the best player in the world. They can't understand why he's up front on his own.

Edna. There are too many overheads at the moment, Matthew, for you to have a car. But keep asking strangers for work. You never know.

Mat.   Maybe this writing will help with that.

Mike. I'll reckon you're upset the punter's against you.

Mat.   After seeing this publisher, I don't know how their minds operate. I suppose, read it; see what you make of it. [*Pauses.*] The hospital's happy the police found me at my flat, not AWOL.

Mike.   Are you dyslexic?

Mat.   No. I need to buy a bigger dictionary.

Lee looked like Marlon Brando wearing his dressing gown with tattered pockets.

Mike.   Oh come on, Lee. New dressing gown needed.

Edna.   Oh come on, you two. Everyone wears a tattered piece of clothing now and then. Just because it has imperfections, doesn't mean you shouldn't wear it. It's still a garment.

I'm a good old-fashioned lady with good morals, Matthew.

Mat.   I have no doubts.

Mike.   You've got a lot of enquiries on the agenda today.

Mat.   Yeah, main one is when I see my support worker.

Edna.   That lady would marry you, but she would never admit it.

Mat.   I wish.

It was nice to see my advocate two hours late.

Edna.   Yes, there was a mix-up in communications. Staff thought you hadn't arrived yet.

Mat.   I'd only been in hospital fifteen hours.

Edna.   Not long enough obviously, Matthew.

Mike.   In for another week then, Mat.

Mat.   Yeah. I'm missing my home-cooked food already.

Edna.   There's nothing more nourishing than home-made dinners, Matthew darling.

Mat.   I need to visit the dentist.

Mike.   You're brave son. I hated the dentist's drill.

Head into town; shoot some pool if you get some leave.

Mat.   I've got other things on my mind.

Edna.   Matthew, today's paper got caught up in today's wind. Can you pick it up, please? It's all over the courtyard.

Mat.   Yes, Edna.

Mike.   Anything decent in the articles today?

Mat.   Haven't read it, Mike.

       I'm going to print some colour copies of my
       writing and get my brother-in-law to pass it round
       his office.

Mike. Ten out of ten for that idea, mate.

Edna. You starting to feel better already?

Mat.   Yes, that corking blonde just started a long shift.

       There's the vicar in the television room. I wonder
       if he's come to bless the hospital.

Mike. Tough job.

Edna. Now, both of you, stop overreacting, please.

Mat.   I don't think they're injecting me today, just
       holding me prisoner.

Edna. That's all they can do at this time.

Mat.   Who's that bus driver waving at me? It's six o'clock
       in the morning – way too early for pleasantries.

Edna. Matthew, it's just a friendly driver trying to cheer
       up your morning.

Mike. When are you sorting out a washing machine for
       your flat?

Edna.   Mike, you know Matthew's short of money at the moment.

Mat.   Can I add that's why I'm writing – for a payday.

Edna.   How did you enjoy your breakfast this morning?

Mat.   A bowl of porridge always goes down well.

Mike.   Let's hope the weather stays at twenty-four degrees today.

Edna.   Yes, it's a beautiful day to lie down on the grass in the fresh air and do some writing.

Mat.   All things considered; after all, I'm in hospital. Yeah, you're right, Edna.

Mike.   You've got the whole summer to play out.

Edna.   That's as pretty as a daisy chain that time on the calendar.

Mat.   Talking of the calendar, it's Father's Day soon. I hope I receive a card.

Edna.   It's always nice when another person acknowledges your existence.

Mat.   Filling a page is exhausting. Another page is in front of you.

Edna.   I think you need to add *mentally*, not *physically*.

Mike. I'm sure they'll realize that, love.

Mat. Mike, went into Nationwide Bank the other day – into their shop front. Talk about the wood framing needing staining.

Mike. Yeah, you'd think, being a bank, they would be able to afford it.

Edna. They have many branches.

Mat. They need a maintenance man. I would do that.

Why me? Why have you given me these powers with eyesight?

Edna. Because you fit the criteria, Matthew, in every way.

Mat. I'm just regaining my senses from the last one.

Edna. Matthew, it has been a long cold bitter winter.

Mat. Sounds like my meetings with the consultants.

I think a change of subject is imminent.

Mike. You can't while you're stuck on section.

Edna. Mike, please stop reminding Matthew of that fact.

Mat. It's better being here now than winter and being stuck indoors all day.

What's the point of a test injection if the consultant doesn't listen to important side effects?

Edna. Let the anger pass quickly.

Mike. That's all you can do.

Mat. Here, Mike, these June mornings are supposed to be mild. I'm cold.

Mike. It's that sunburn from yesterday. The sun got you from behind the clouds.

Edna. It's okay, Matthew. Your days are numbered for this visit to hospital.

Mat. Yeah, I should be using some swear words about this situation.

Mike. Yeah, I agree.

Edna. Your writing really doesn't warrant swear words.

Mat. I guess you're right. Swearing's not very attractive.

Mike. Edna's the one wearing the trousers, mate. What she says goes.

Edna. Just keeping it civilized. I want this in a refined and educated manner so the story can develop with interest.

Mat. That's the arrangement I want to achieve if possible.

I'll try to articulate in expressing amusement.

Mike. Sounds serious. A chuckle is better than nothing.

Edna. Sounds fantastic, Matthew.

Mike. You always like complimenting Mat. Don't you, dear?

Edna. Matthew, you're filled with enthusiasm.

Mat. Yes, I've been inspired by the sunshine of the last couple of days.

Mike. Sunshine always brings out the best in people. Edna. Matthew's at his best all the time as far as I'm concerned.

Mat. Thank you. You're really starting to grow on me now.

Edna. Like a colourful flower that blooms in the summer.

Mike. Hey, you two are making great poetry together. It's flowing like a river.

Mat. This isn't an experiment on my poetic skills, Mike.

Mike. Okay, mate. I'm only saying.

Edna. Don't be too harsh on him, Matthew, please.

Mat. I'm not having a go, Mike.

Edna. Gentlemen, shake hands and make up.

Mat. I think you're blowing the disagreement out of proportion.

Mike. Everything's fine, love. Stop worrying.

Edna. It's okay, Matthew. We just have different opinions on the matter.

Mike. Can I get a word in edgeways please?

Mat. Don't get too downhearted, Mike. No offence.

Can we change the subject?

Edna. Both of you, start on the television stand for the front room.

Mike. We still need materials before we can start the job, darling.

Mat. I think I'm going to order some pizza. Two for the price of one offers in the local shop.

Edna. Yeah, sounds like a bargain deal.

Mike. Yeah, I'll have some of that, mate.

Edna. This is the only time. You know I like to promote home cooking.

Mat. I'm perplexed about how to fix this shelf up.

Mike. You have to call in a carpenter who knows what he's doing.

Edna. It's nothing you can't achieve yourself, Matthew.

Mat. It is an awkward job – floating shelf, made out of floor joists, timber eight by four, very large-scale production.

Edna. A wonderful offer from your sister and husband with this furniture they're presenting you.

Mike. Yeah, there are some nice pieces there.

Mat. No one's going to be interested in reading about these kinds of happenings.

Edna. You'll be surprised, Matthew.

Mike. If you don't write, you don't know.

Mat. That's Norman shouting up at my window.

Mike. See what he wants.

Mat. He wants help moving a millstone. What's Norman think, I'm the world's strongest man? That I can carry that millstone on my own?

Mike. Lucky you could roll it.

Edna. Matthew, that was well within your capability. You just proved it.

Mat. Lovely setting for a few tins of beer at the high rocks looking out over the views.

Edna. Yes, spectacular landscape down in the valley.

Mike. Yeah, I agree.

Mat. Amazing how a phone call out of the blue can cheer you up.

Edna. That's right, my dear.

Mike. You happy to speak to Ethan?

Mat. I don't know what to do with my life. I've put in nearly fifty applications for jobs and nothing.

Edna. Sometimes, life is like that when you get older. You just need a break, Matthew.

Mike. You got this now, mate.

Mat. I've been asking people for work up at the shops with no results. It's breaking my spirit.

There's that tall girl for upstairs.

Mike. Lean out the window, and tell her the event that took place.

Edna. Just because you fancy her, Matthew.

Mat. Yes, she's gorgeous. Bumped into her upstairs ten minutes ago. She was taking the dog out.

Mike. Remember, it's later in the day that you feel the benefits of not smoking.

Edna. It's a hard task. So if you fail, always remember each moment can be a new moment.

Mat. Thank you, Edna. You always calm the situation down. Why can't I get rid of this tense feeling?

Mike. It's just the way life is panning out at this time.

Mat. I need these injections phased out so I can clear my head.

Edna. Don't worry, Matthew. Everything will be fine in time.

Mat. There's the post. Which bailiff is it this time?

Edna. It's not the lovely postman's fault. He's just delivering the letter.

Matthew, it's only a few years away from you gaining financial stability of your own.

Mat.   My handwriting isn't great. It's embarrassing showing it to people.

Edna.   When you print this out on the computer, no one will know the difference.

Mat.   You're always positive in heaven. That's what I like.

Mike.   Change the subject. I'm listening to you and my wife.

Mat.   This isn't a play, as you know.

Mike.   No, it's a sketch, mate.

Edna.   And a wonderful one at that.

Mat.   Unbelievable, people may be reading this after they've paid for it.

Edna.   Now come on, Matthew. You're not doing this for financial gain.

Mike.   Of course he is, love.

Mat.   Not sure why I put the pen down for so long.

Edna.   You've been sidetracked, Matthew. You're back on course now though.

Mike.   Yeah, I enjoy these three-way conversations.

Mat.   Helps pass time, mate. Problem is, I'm getting writer's cramp.

Edna.   It's a unique idea, refreshing.

Mat.   Who's going to play you two when the play directors start circling?

Edna.   Yes, you better get a solicitor – get the idea patented.

Mike.   Won't be difficult, mate.

Mat.   Am I allowed to mention the orbs you display to me?

Edna.   Yes, it's no big secret. You're not the only one who sees them.

Mat.   You're such a nice kind spirit, Edna.

Edna.   You get the wings wrapped around your vision for that gesture.

Mat.   How long are they going to be working outside? They were here for months in the summer.

Mike.   How do I know? You'll have to find out yourself.

Edna.   Yes, it does disturb the peace, them banging away all day.

Mat.   I wonder what event is going to inspire the next sentence.

Mike. Who knows, mate? None of us can predict the future.

Edna. That may not be true, Matthew. We may be able to.

Mat. I personally wouldn't bet against it.

I'll tell them about the orb cluster that appeared in my front room about seven years ago, before we had talked.

Edna. We were making it so obvious that we were there; it wasn't the right time to talk.

Mike. Yeah, I even dropped that rubber out of thin air right in front of you.

Mat. I remember it clearly. Really took me by surprise.

Mike. You're more blessed than most psychics. I'll tell you that.

Mat. Yeah, those metallic silver orbs that just appear are tremendous. They really opened my eyes to you being there.

Edna. Yes, it was our easiest form of communication at that point.

Mat. If I become prosperous, I can go to the dentist and get two real teeth and get rid of this plate.

Edna. Yes, prices for dentistry nowadays are shocking.

Mike. Yeah, I had one of those when I was alive. Irritating, aren't they?

Mat. How about my nan reaching the golden age of one hundred?

Edna. Yes, it's a big milestone.

Mike. Not many make it to that age.

Edna. Did she receive a telegram from the queen?

Mat. Yes she did, but they rang up checking every week leading up to her birthday, making sure it was okay to send it.

Mike. That was to making sure she was still alive.

Edna. Matthew, why don't you go out for a walk? It's a beautiful sunny day.

Mat. I've got blisters from walking all those miles yesterday.

Mike. You only walked into Tunbridge Wells and back.

Edna. If you had MOTed your car, the police wouldn't have scrapped it.

Yeah well, failing it on a seat belt that worked was a bit harsh.

Mike. I thought that, Mat.

Mat.   Edna, can I ask you your age? Or is that prying in your business?

Edna. It's no problem. You can ask my age. I was seventy-four when I passed.

Mat.   Edna, if somebody reads this and connects the dots, they might seek me out.

Mike. It's a possibility they may do, mate.

Mat.   Hey, these bad beats on Poker Heaven are no good. All in on Ace King after the flop, and he gets a runner – clubs for a flush.

Edna. Going back to what you were saying, they will only know you as Mat.

Mike. A rest from Poker Heaven will do you good anyway, mate.

Mat.   Do you know what I like about this idea?

Edna. No, Matthew.

Mat.   It's polite and child friendly, so it will cater to all generations.

Mike. That's right; no swearing or promoting drugs.

Mat. Edna, who do you think is going to win the big fight?

Edna. I think it's brutal and barbaric.

Mat. How long does this have to stay top secret?

Mike. Well, mate, until you have enough material.

Mat. There's a lot to memorise already.

Edna. Not for the professionals, Matthew.

Mat. Did you support a football team when you were on earth?

Mike. Yeah, Fulham.

Mat. Now the sky TV's fitted, I can watch Bob Marley's Rainbow concert; top performance.

Edna. Yes, I like Bob Marley.

Mat. Writing this is starting to break my spirit.

Edna. Oh please, Matthew; it would take more than that to break your spirit.

Mat. Yeah, I know. I'm just feeling sorry for myself at the moment.

Mike. Feeling sorry for yourself doesn't help, mate.

Edna. Mike, please be a touch more supportive.

Mike. Yeah, sorry, darling.

Mat. Pie mash peas for dinner.

Edna. I used to love that dinner when I was alive.

Mike. Online poker will keep you penniless, you know?

Mat. I don't play it that often.

Edna. Mike's just warning you for the future.

Mike. My mates and I used to like a friendly game.

Edna. So, forty years old now – middle aged.

Mat. Yep, my youth has gone forever.

Mike. Plenty of years left yet, mate.

Edna. Yes, you have your whole life ahead of you.

Mat. What about when I become famous for writing this book?

Edna. Your luck will change.

Mat. Look at that bloke in the convertible. His head must be frozen. It's winter for god's sake.

Edna. Maybe he's enjoying the brisk winter air.

Mike.   Rather him than you, mate.

Mat.   Yeah, I would rather wear a beanie hat.

Edna.   Matthew, you're such a wimp.

Mat.   People need to know I don't do psychic readings.

Mike.   None of your family has asked for one since you told them.

Edna.   I think it fell on deaf ears, Matthew.

Mat.   I don't believe they believe me.

Edna.   Maybe they will if this hits the Internet.

Mike.   Oi, Mat.

Mat.   Do you want to ask me a question, Mike?

Mike.   Nah.

Mat.   Breakdown in communications there, mate. Sorry.

Edna.   It's bound to happen.

Mat.   Edna, you're not your usual bright and breezy self tonight.

Edna.   Use longer words and you'll fill the pages up more quickly.

Mat.   I'm going to start taking the pad out with me. I'm missing so many chances to jot down ideas.

Edna. Don't let it take over your life that much, Matthew.

Mat.   It's all I've been thinking about since I picked the pen back up.

Mike. Ideas pop in and out, mate. I know what you mean.

Mat.   Aw, ran out of cigarettes.

Edna. You'll have to cope without.

Mike. I'm sure you can last the evening.

Edna. Maybe people's perception will be that you're some kind of rapper like Eminem.

Mat.   I wouldn't mind his trappings under the radar.

       I need to decide what I'm going to buy Ethan for Christmas.

Edna. You need to explain who people are briefly.

Mat.   Ethan's my son.

       Mike, did I tell you the poor lad's got a confidence problem because of a hairy mole on his face?

Mike. Yeah, that's funny, mate.

Edna. You two, don't be so horrible. Have some compassion for the poor lad.

Mat. Hey, it's quite peaceful writing by candlelight.

Edna. Yes the flickering of the flames makes for a peaceful ambience.

Mat. How do I know you're in heaven and not from another plant in the universe?

Mike. You don't, mate.

Edna. We had this conversation two years ago.

Mat. Mike, that bird with the long curly hair who works in the local shop is a corker.

Edna. Yes, she's beautiful isn't she, Matthew?

Mike. He was talking to me, love.

Mat. I'm going to wander up to the village and get some cigarettes.

Mike. Didn't think you would wait a night.

Mat. I bet diving for gold is a right buzz.

Edna. When you find the mother lode, Matthew.

Mat. I might get back into doing my weightlifting today.

Edna. Yes, you should keep your muscles pumped up for the ladies.

Mat. I might get Katy to dye my hair today. I'm starting to look grey.

Mike. What are you – a woman? That's their treatment.

Mat. I'm getting a complex about how old I'm looking.

Edna. That's what happens when you get older, Matthew.

Mike. When you going to finish your decorating?

Edna. The plans are still on the table.

Mat. Yeah, that's right, Edna. I'll get round to it. Haven't decided what colours will be used yet.

Mike. You've been stretching this job out for ages.

Mat. Are you saying I'm lazy?

I'm juggling the idea of getting a pet dog, Mike.

Mike. Yeah, why not? It'd get you out for some exercise.

Edna. They can make a mess of your home.

Mat. Yeah, Roxanne chewed up my walls when I looked after her.

Edna. They are beautiful creatures and very loyal.

Mat.   Shall I mention some of these cloud visions you've shown me?

Edna. Yes, not all of them, slow release, please.

Mat.   An amazing carved angelfish floating over Manor Road; I knew it was an angelfish. It was a carbon copy of the fish I had in my fish tank.

Mike. People are going to have trouble believing you on that one.

Edna. It's up to them.

Mat.   That's no big deal. I know what I saw.

       How do I go about getting this published?

Edna. You'll have to find a publisher who deals with free style.

Mat.   Chris says I should self-publish.

Mike. He was taking the Mickey out of you.

Mat.   That man who had to wear the iron mask must have been horrible.

Edna. Yes, very strange punishment for a human being.

Mat.   Mike, do you want to comment on that?

Mike. Yeah, it would be pretty irritating.

Don't worry about your rough writing. When it's completed and printed out from the computer, who's going to know?

Edna. Your *a*'s look like triangles.

Mat. Free-handing on your knee isn't easy.

Edna. Matthew, if you start your weightlifting again, be careful not to put your weight bar through the ceiling.

Mat. I'll be careful this time. I've run out of filler.

Mike. You are tall, so it's not your fault.

Mat. Mike, they're coming round to fit me a new bathroom.

Mike. Are they?

Mat. I don't need a new bathroom. What a waste of money.

Mike. That's the council for you.

Mat. That woman who I told I was writing a book asked how it was going a couple of days back.

Edna. She's a lovely lady. I think she likes you.

Mat. I get that sense. But she's a friend's girlfriend.

Can you channel in some sentences, just to help me push on?

Edna. No, Matthew, it all has to come naturally from your own mind.

Mat. Thanks for bringing out the sense of humour in me, guys.

Edna. Sure, some people will find this funny.

Mike. Don't underestimate yourself, mate.

Mat. It's fascinating waiting and wondering.

Where did you guys set up residence in England?

Mike. In Haylesford, Birmingham.

Mat. I've heard of Haylesford. It rings a bell.

Edna. They have a football team.

Mat. Not in the top leagues.

Edna. what music did you like?

Edna. Beethoven's Ninth Symphony.

Mat. Classical was your favourite.

Edna. Yes, it was, Matthew.

Mat.   I might enter a free roll on Poker Heaven.

Mike. Yeah, saves your money playing those tournaments.

Edna. I'm against gambling. A fool and his money soon part ways on those websites.

Mike. Anything else you want to know about us, mate?

Mat.   Not at the moment, Mike, Another day I'm sure I'll ask.

I better get this flat tidied up; it hasn't been done for a few days.

Edna. Yes, best to keep on top of it.

Mike. Yeah, it's a chore.

Mat.   So, is reincarnation true then, Edna?

Edna. I couldn't possibly answer that question, Matthew, not on paper anyway.

Mike. Don't get me involved in this one, mate.

Mat.   Properly not looking forward to this winter.

Edna. Yes, these bleak cold days can't compare to the summer.

Mike. Yeah, I prefer the summer – more daylight.

Edna. Writing inspires more writing.

Mat. Yeah, starting a new page. You wonder what's going to fill this one?

Mike. I bet no one can guess.

Mat. It's harder and harder to keep the reader entertained.

Edna. Yes, Matthew, you have to keep the public interested.

Mat. Sausages and jacket potatoes went down nicely.

Edna. Yes, it's a good traditional English supper.

Mike. Hey, Mat, why don't you walk into town tomorrow, see what's happening?

Mat. Nothing's going on in town.

Edna. You have to make your own happenings.

Mat. How? I'm broke.

Edna. It doesn't cost to window shop, my darling.

Mat. Jehovah's Witnesses will find it an uncomfortable read.

Mike. It will go with their morbid beliefs.

Edna. They're still human beings; remember that.

Mike. We do, love, but still it's morbid what they preach.

Mat. Maybe I should start reading some of my books, generate some ideas.

Edna. Why don't you get *The Mammoth Encyclopedia of Extraterrestrial Encounters*?

Mike. What are you going to find in that?

Mat. I bought that book when I had my own UFO sighting.

Edna. When did you see a UFO, Matthew?

Mat. Years ago, flying across the sky.

Mike. Are you sure your description's right – that it was a UFO?

Mat. Don't know; it was going too fast. I couldn't focus on it.

They're talking about eating horse meat. I've never tried it.

Edna. I think horses should be left alone.

Mike. Yeah, they're pets in this country. We're not in France.

Mat. I might get my sister to do a session of reflexology on my feet.

Edna. Yes, I used to love having that done.

Mike. That's for pansies, mate.

Mat. Yeah whatever, Mike.

Looks like we're getting annoyed with each other, Mike.

Mike. Not at all, mate. Friends for life.

Mat. I've got to think of a title for this book.

Mike. What have you come up with so far?

Mat. Mat, Mike, Edna – six different combinations if you mix the names around.

Edna. Those are some for the short list.

Mat. I don't like the way that electric fire is making that hissing noise.

Edna. No, it's very dangerous using it with broken tubes.

Mike. I'll agree with that, mate.

Edna. This is the story of your life.

Mat. Not just mine; it's about you two as well.

Mike. No one knows how long you've waited for this moment, when you can print out.

Edna. I always new you had what it takes.

Mat.   Nothing out there but blue sky, Edna.

Edna. And a cold wind.

Mat.   Who keeps leaving piles of rubbish and fridges outside the flats?

Edna. You'll have to enquire with some of your neighbours.

Mike. Yeah, don't ask us, mate.

Mat.   What if people decide you're not real and I've made you up? Would they still have the same interest?

Edna. Yes, I think they will, Matthew.

Mat.   I wonder whether people find it strange the way you're standing next to me. Why me?

Edna. Because you prayed to be psychic.

Mike. Your prayers were answered, mate.

Edna. Women love to hear man's insecurities; it gives them something to work on.

Mat.   I'll keep that in mind, Edna.

Mike. You can't just talk about your life in one go, mate.

Mat.   You guys have been around since I was a boy; that's a lot of years.

Edna. There's way too much for you to remember in one attempt.

Mat.   Shame I had to burn five pads worth when the police were smashing my door in.

Edna. Yes, you were paranoid then with mental health services on your case at the same time.

Mike. You were carrying a sports bag with your writing inside it at that point.

Mat.   I thought they wanted to know what was in the bag. That's what spooked me.

Edna. You've had to start from scratch; it's put you back months.

Mat.   It's in the past now. I didn't want anyone reading those pages.

I told Ethan I was getting a book together. He witnessed all that writing. He must be wondering where it all went.

Edna. You let him know you've started again.

Mat.   It's getting tricky to remember what I have and haven't mentioned.

Edna. We can always remind you.

Mat. You've got big memories, you guys.

Edna. I'm not a guy, Matthew.

Mat. Cars are frosted over this morning.

Edna. Yes, a lot of windscreens will be scraped.

Mat. Mike, are you awake this morning?

Mike. Yeah, I'm awake, mate.

Mat. Mike, I see you in a vision wearing a flat cap. Is that the hat you wore in life?

Mike. Yes, I liked the granddad cap.

Mat. I had one of those when I was a boy.

Edna. They're meant for old people really.

Mat. I was a mod.

With all this paperwork, I'll need to hire a receptionist.

Edna. Yes, you're not very experienced on the computer.

Mat. Even after all these years, because I can't see you, it's a strange feeling.

Edna. Yes, but you have no doubt we're here.

Mat. No. When Paul and I were talking about him seeing the light after his motorbike crash, his crutch suddenly fell over surprising both of us. I'd told him spirits were real before that.

Mat. How old were you when you passed, Mike?

Mike. Sixty-four, mate.

Edna. I sense it's going to be a good writing day today.

Mat. I hope so. I'm in a rush to finish this pad now.

Mike. You've got to think about it, mate.

Mat. They're going to be puzzled as to whether or not you two are real.

Edna. I don't think there's any doubt we're here with you.

Mike. Oh come on, love. You're always going to get the sceptics; that's just part of life.

Mat. I had to laugh when my mum said Ethan had seen a ghost.

Edna. Matthew, if Ethan saw a ghost, it would be scary for him.

Mike. Yeah, remember, he's only fourteen.

Mat.   These days as a writer can seem awfully long.

Edna. Yes, Matthew, but it's a small amount of time in the scheme of things.

Mike. Yeah, that's right, mate.

Mat.   There's todays post. Bet it's the water board wanting some money.

Edna. Yes, everyone's after your money nowadays.

Mike. It is your debt though, mate.

Mat.   Edna I'm thankful for this blessing heaven's given me.

Edna. You're a decent chap. That's why.

Mike. I'll echo that, dear.

Mat.   I wouldn't mind meeting a woman.

Edna. Oh, Matthew, you don't need a woman. You're better off isolated when you're writing.

Mike. Come on, love. He wants some female company.

Mat.   At least my thoughts aren't going to waste now.

Mike. Nah, that's right, mate.

Mat.   Okay, time to put the kettle on.

Edna. Yes, your mind's entitled to a tea break.

Mat. I need a washing machine. Lugging the wash up to the laundrette is a hassle.

Edna. Yes, you haven't had one since Brad from across the road kindly helped you throw your old one out.

Mat. Yeah, I like Brad, but that was months ago.

Some people are scared of ghosts, aren't they?

Edna. Not all ghosts are friendly.

Mike. Come on, love.

Mat. Shall we change the subject to something lighter?

Edna. Yes, I think that would be a good idea.

Quite a wad of papers you're accumulating now, Matthew.

Mat. Are you impressed with my wad, Edna?

Mike. You don't have to answer that, dear.

Mat. You two are the nicest spirits I could have met.

Edna. That's a wonderful compliment. Thank you.

Mike. Yeah, cheers, mate; it's a pleasure helping you.

Mat. Those joss sticks give off a cool aroma.

Edna. A nice present from your sister.

Mike. Not something I would have used.

Mat.   I'll ring my mum later, see if there's a roast dinner going.

Mike. Yeah, I'd go with that.

Edna. Your mum does a lovely Sunday roast.

Mat.   Unusual sight seeing that bubble car flipped over this morning.

Edna. Probably a gang of drunken youths.

Mike. We all did stupid things like that when we were growing up.

Mat.   Why are you getting shy when I ask if you have any questions, Edna?

Edna. Channelling stopped for the time.

Mike. We are here to help him as well, love.

Mat.   You're being stern this morning, Edna.

Edna. Matthew, I don't mean to upset you in any way, darling.

Mat.   It's warmed up a bit today.

Edna. Yes, it's not midwinter yet.

Mike. Yeah, you wait for January and February.

Mat. I'm not looking forward to those months.

Clare's nervous. She's doing her first lesbian club meeting.

Edna. Oh, Matthew, why are you telling us that?

Mike. Because he wants to go, love.

Mat. It's for women only.

I might get myself a mountain bike.

Mike. Wrong time of year, mate.

Edna. Yes you need to buy hats and gloves for riding through winter's cold winds.

Mat. Edna, can you do that vision where you wrap your angel wings around me that always warms me up?

Edna. Aw, that's very sweet of you.

Mike. Those wings are for me, mate, not you.

Mat. Are you sure all this small talk is going to keep people interested?

Edna. It's hardly small talk – me wrapping my wings around you.

Mike. You have to remember, it's second nature to Mat having us around.

Mat. What's the conversation going to be like when I meet a publisher? I'm going to have to mention being psychic.

Edna. The way you've been treated by mental health services, I'm not surprised you have some apprehension.

Mike. All smoke and mirrors, they think.

Mat. I don't want people to think I'm some kind of professional writer.

Edna. It's for the amazement and mundane.

Mike. Yeah, it can't all be sensational.

Mat. Just imagine if hundreds of people start reading it.

Mike. I reckon that many will be interested.

Edna. Matthew, you're wanting too much too soon.

Would you not call us ghosts or ghouls? It's insulting, Matthew.

Mike. Spirits is fine, 'cause that's what we are.

Mat.   No problem, guys. That means the title of the book has to change.

Mike. There's Scott. Grab some fags off him.

Mat.   Yeah, he's always borrowing stuff from me.

Edna. Yes, I'm sure Scott won't mind.

Mike. Have you forgotten you're supposed to be giving up cigarettes?

Mat.   I have cut down.

How can I concentrate on my book with them singing that "Wheels on the Bus" nursery rhyme?

Mike. You didn't plan on the mothers meeting in the library.

Edna. Mothers need somewhere warm to take the babies.

Mat.   I'm not complaining.

       It's a good feeling getting the first pages printed out.

Edna. Yes, that's the first couple out of the way.

Mike. Yeah, nice job, mate.

Mat.   It's quite cheap to get all of this ready and organised to send off.

Mike. That's lucky, mate, because you aren't well off.

Edna. You don't have to rub it in, Mike.

Mike. Oh come on, love. I'm not taking the Mickey out of him.

Mat. No offence taken.

As for those ideas you were putting into your database, can I log into some of them?

Edna. You've done it all by yourself so far. Why do you need my help now?

Mike. It's not as easy as that, mate.

Mat. I was doing that channelling writing last year.

Edna. That wasn't for profit though, Matthew.

Mat. Mike, have a word with her, will you?

Mike. There's nothing I can do. Each to his or her own.

Edna. Stop trying to make divisions between me and Mike please, Matthew. It won't work.

Mat. I nearly laughed out loud in the library. Those mums would have thought I was mad.

Edna. You have to remember that people don't know we exist.

Mat.   We've been talking so long now I forget.

Mike. Yeah, it's easy to forget.

Mat.   Edna, you know that morning when there were four rainbows in the valley? Was that your projection?

Edna. Yes, it was, Matthew?

Mat.   I thought so. I've never seen a rainbow so large in scale; unbelievable powers heaven has.

Mike. Why's it taken you so long to ask? That happened a couple of years ago.

Mat.   A lot happened in those days.

Mat.   Am I the only one who can see them?

Edna. Yes.

Mat.   That explains why I never read about it. I thought someone would have taken a photo of the massive one.

Edna. It wasn't there in anyone else's eyesight.

Mat.   I could see the end of the rainbow.

Mike. The sceptics will have trouble buying that.

Mat.   Yeah, I do know rainbows are circular; that's why I thought it was strange that I could see the end.

Shame Paul Collins life came to an end. I miss our poker nights.

Edna.   Yes, mucker man. I know you miss him. He sends his regards with a handshake.

Mat.   Please pass on a message. Life's not the same without him.

Edna.   Consider it done, Matthew.

Mat.   It's like the adult version of Harry Potter. That or am I in another world?

Edna.   No, it is mysterious.

Mat.   How many books do you think I should write?

Mike.   I reckon about five.

Edna.   Five should be ample.

Mat.   It's a daunting task.

What about that time you turned my bedroom ceiling into our solar system? How did you do that?

Edna.   That's heaven's trade secret. You wouldn't understand.

Mike. Yeah, sorry, mate.

Mat. It was a spectacular illusion.

Are you old spirits or are you newly departed?

Edna. Newly departed as you put it.

Mat. Do you have kids alive on earth now?

Edna. Yes, we have. That's enough questions about us for the time being.

Mat. I might pop up to the café for a late breakfast.

Edna. Yes it's important to support local restaurants.

Mike. Every customer counts.

Edna. Don't start slacking now. You're on a roll.

Mat. Just thinking of something.

Mike. Yeah, you don't want to be jotting down any old rubbish.

Mat. Who's projecting those images? Is it you or someone else?

Edna. Who do you think it is, Matthew?

Mat. I don't know. That's why I am asking.

Mike. It's us doing them, mate.

Mat. To explain what these images look like, I call them visions because they look like a television screen. But not all of them – some look like computer graphics.

Mike. Basically, we can copy any image known to humankind, mate.

Mat. I'll vouch for that. I see them all the time.

Mike. People are going to want to know more about these visions.

Edna. Yes they will, Matthew. I'll confirm that.

Mat. So are there rules about getting into heaven?

Edna. Yes there are, Matthew.

Mike. You've got to be a kind spirit to get in, mate.

Mat. I didn't like seeing that old lady lying spreadeagled on the ground.

Edna. Yes, it was a nasty fall. Plus temperatures are freezing.

Mike. Yeah, poor old dear. I hope she's all right.

Firework Night was a good night out.

Mat.   Yeah it was. I enjoyed that, aside from the rain.

Edna.   Yes, there's a friendly community spirit to those nights.

Mat.   Had a chat with a publisher. Did you hear, Edna?

Edna.   Of course I did.

Mike.   She was a nice lady, but it's not the company you'll be dealing with.

Mat.   My cousin Ben has offered to swap my computer for his car. What do you reckon, Mike?

Mike.   You can't swap your computer. You need it for e-mails.

Edna.   It's a non-starter.

Mat.   There's times when I wonder why people should be interested in my life. Then I remember I have heaven channelled into me.

Edna.   It's a fascinating subject.

Mike.   I said it before. Sceptics will be crawling all over you.

Edna.   Come on, it's not going to be that bad.

Mat.   You're quite sure of yourself, Edna.

Edna. A woman always knows best.

Mike. Yeah, in your dreams, love.

Mat.   It's getting a bit too down to earth now. You sound like an earthling couple.

It's very quiet without the television on. I'm used to music playing in the background.

Edna. Yes, it's peaceful and tranquil.

Mike. You're left with only your own thoughts.

They're going to think you're proper old school – writing with pen and pad.

Edna. Most people go on Facebook now to write their life stories.

Mike. Yeah, I suppose most people would type it straight on a computer.

Edna. Writing it down keeps your mind ticking over.

Mat.   My mum told me not to give up my day job hoping this writing will be successful.

Edna. Yes, she wasn't very encouraging.

Mat.   She did break out in a smile after reading some of it.

Mike. She's a sceptic, mate.

Mat. I should show her this page.

Mike. She has only read a few pages; I'll give her that.

Edna. Mike's being a bit harsh. Don't take any notice.

Mat. Do you miss the pub, Mike?

Mike. Got 'em up here, mate.

Mat. People aren't going to have that.

Edna. The choice is theirs, Matthew.

Mat. Who's dumping suitcases in the car park, for god's sake?

Edna. You might as well just put it in the bin for the dustman.

Mike. You going to check and see if there's money or something of value inside?

Mat. No, I don't think so. It's in a big puddle of water.

It's a good feeling not being stuck in reverse gear.

Edna. You can thank the hospital for that. They inspired you to pick up the pen and start writing.

Mike. At least one good thing came out of it.

Mat. Yes, it was a blessing in disguise.

Edna. Of course the hospital will beg to differ.

Mat. Scott says you need over thirty thousand words for a manuscript to be classed as a book.

Edna. Yes, that's right.

Mike. Yeah, you've got a way to go yet.

Edna. Matthew dear, why don't you browse the Internet for a different publisher?

Mike. Try to find one in England; the other company was based in America.

Mat. It's getting exciting the closer we get to the next stage.

Edna. There's still a long way to go yet.

Mike. Come on, love. Don't make it sound too daunting.

Mat. So they will be fitting a new bathroom in my flat.

Edna. Matthew, make your writing smaller. I know you're trying to fill the pages more quickly.

Mike. Give him a break, love. That Impact pen he's writing with has a big nib.

Mat.   Those adult-sized onesies – are people seriously wearing those out in the streets?

Edna. They look like big babies.

Mike. I don't think you would see a builder wearing one on site.

Mat.   I've just seen Katy in one; she looks like a frog.

Leaves are stripped of the trees now.

Edna. Yes, winter's settling in for the long haul.

Mike. Don't remind him, love – three months of coldness.

Mat.   My sister says there's snow on the way.

Edna. I used to love snow when I was a child.

Mike. Yeah, building snowmen is good fun.

Mat.   We built a Rastaman with dreadlocks. He looked more like a robot – six-foot wide rocks and boulders with a square head.

       Do you know what, Edna? I'm fed up with being broke.

Edna. Money's everything when you haven't got it.

Mike. Yeah, it's always the way, mate.

You've got tons of knowledge in your head.

Edna. Don't underestimate yourself.

Mat. Thanks for the encouragement. I think my future lies in the pen.

How do you win over sceptics?

Edna. You can't win over every sceptic. Some will stay as they are.

Mat. If I was to say what song sums up my story, I would say "Earthquake" by Labyrinth and Tinie Tempah.

Edna. Yes, that's our anthem tune.

Mike. Yeah, that's a real banger, that tune.

Edna. Are you excited about the first person reading your work?

Mat. Not thinking that far ahead.

Mike. You should do, mate. You've nearly finished book one of five.

Edna. Yes, you can brace yourself for positive feedback.

Mat. Let's hope so.